Great teachers access their inner values, drive, and talents to holistically support all students. They hold their passion for bettering the lives of students deep within their souls and pour all of who they are into their craft. This book embodies how, through connection to their own beliefs, Christian educators can broaden their impact on the lives of the students, families, and colleagues they support.

—Shelly Rosene, instructional coach

This beautiful book is a reminder that teaching is so much more than a career choice; it is a calling from God. The text expertly weaves anecdotes, scripture, and practical classroom application to create an edifying tapestry of inspiration for the teacher's heart. If you are facing burnout, this book will be a gift from God directly to your spirit. I believe it will be uplifting and encouraging to countless educators, and thus a blessing to their students!

—Rachel Jorgenson, author of *Supporting Your Child with Special Needs* and *Loving Your Job in Special Education*

In a world where you can be anything, be kind. We never know the battles that anyone is facing and we want to treat others with kindness and shine God's light. God gives us all the gift of life and guides us to our purpose in this world. We want to encourage and help others to fulfill their purpose. When you expect more, you achieve more! This little light of mine, I'm gonna let it shine! Shine! Shine! Shine!

—Melissa Hayes, Professor/Director of Special Education

We are fully known and perfectly loved by our heavenly Father. This book is full of helpful ideas on how educators can make their students feel known and loved. There are so many things outside of your control as an educator; this book helps you focus on the things inside your circle of control and ultimately points you back to the one who is in complete control.

—Patrick Stiner, educator

As educators, we often get overwhelmed with all of the demands of being a teacher. This book has helped me remember that I am called to be in the classroom and to make sure every student knows they are loved and cared for, no matter their circumstances. *Seeing Your Students through God's Eyes* has encouraged me to build strong connections with other Christian educators so we can celebrate, pray, collaborate, and support each other through all of the challenges of being an educator.

—Anna Appecelli, educator

SEEING *Your* STUDENTS *Through* GOD'S EYES

ALYSSA STICKAN

WESTBOW
PRESS®
A DIVISION OF THOMAS NELSON
& ZONDERVAN

The Holy Bible, English Standard Version. ESV® Text
Edition: 2016. Copyright © 2001 by Crossway Bibles, a
publishing ministry of Good News Publishers.

WestBow Press books may be ordered through booksellers or by contacting:

WestBow Press
A Division of Thomas Nelson & Zondervan
1663 Liberty Drive
Bloomington, IN 47403
www.westbowpress.com
844-714-3454

ISBN: 979-8-3850-2482-7 (sc)
ISBN: 979-8-3850-2483-4 (e)

Library of Congress Control Number: 2024908833

Print information available on the last page.

WestBow Press rev. date: 05/22/2024

CONTENTS

DEDICATION

To my husband, Lucas, who has supported me and
believed in me before I believed in myself.

PRAYER OF BLESSING

Heavenly Father, in the pursuit of becoming a better educator, I humbly come before You with an earnest prayer. I desire to be a vessel of Your love, kindness, and wisdom in the lives of the students I serve and my colleagues. Grant me the strength to exemplify the virtues of patience, understanding, and compassion as I navigate the intricate journey of education.

I open my heart to Your guidance, seeking wisdom from the pages of this book as a source of inspiration and enlightenment. Use its teachings to illuminate my understanding of how to connect with each student on a deeper level, to tailor my lessons to their needs, and to impart knowledge with grace and humility.

In Your holy name, I offer this prayer, trusting that with Your grace, I can be the educator You've called me to be.

Amen.

CHAPTER 1

MY STORY

Every child deserves a champion—an adult who will never give up on them, who understands the power of connection and insists that they become the best that they can possibly be.

– Rita Pierson

The field of education is constantly evolving; with innovative teaching methodologies, technological advancements, and evolving pedagogical approaches transforming the way we educate the next generation. Amid all this chaos, we can forget what is truly important in life. We get sucked into the frustrations and drama that occur at school, and often we forget to stop and pray. With everything we are juggling, it's necessary to take a step back and turn to prayer. It's crucial to pray for our students—their academic growth, their family life, and their aspirations. Additionally, we should pray for our relationships with our colleagues–that they may recognize the good within their students and that they may have positive mental and emotional well-being. Additionally, we need to relinquish control and allow God to lead us on the right path. We need to accept that our plans may not always align with

His, and trust in His greater purpose for us. Let us never forget that we are all God's beloved children, and we should always strive to spread His light and love to those around us.

> Let go and let God have his way in your life, and He will bless you exceedingly, abundantly, above all that you can ask or think. (Ephesians 3:20)

With an alarming increase in burnout rates among teachers, the need for remembering the positive is more important than ever.[1] Teaching is more than just a profession; it is a calling, a vocation that many individuals pursue with a deep sense of purpose and dedication. Teachers choose to enter into education because they desire to make a difference in the lives of others. They believe that one teacher can change the lives of many students. Teachers know that the work is hard and that oftentimes the pay doesn't compare to other available jobs, but they are called to teaching. They are called to raising the next generation. This calling is a passion. A passion for helping others, a passion for teaching a subject, a passion for sharing knowledge, a drive to help students be better tomorrow than they were yesterday. This drive is why teachers get into teaching.

Despite this passion, teachers often find themselves grappling with frustration and overwhelming teaching environments, leading to a decline in their love for both the job and their students. The education system is experiencing a massive increase of teacher burnout right now. Teacher burnout is a complex and pervasive issue, with heavy workloads, administrative pressures, classroom management challenges, and academic standards contributing to the problem. The emotional and mental toll

---

[1] Less than 70% of teachers made it to their fifth year of teaching in 2022 compared to 87% in 2019. (2023 PELSB)

of these challenges can slowly erode the initial enthusiasm that brought educators into the profession.

In the face of these difficulties, it is crucial for educators to reflect on the profound impact that they can have on their students' lives. Dedicated teachers go beyond simply imparting subject matter knowledge, instead additionally serving as mentors, role models, and sources of inspiration for the next generation. The lessons taught in the classroom extend far beyond academic skills, encompassing crucial life skills, values, and a love for learning that can shape the course of students' lives.

While it is important to acknowledge the challenges teachers face, it is equally essential to recognize the positive influence that they have on their students. Moments of connection, understanding, and encouragement can leave indelible marks on students' lives, shaping their futures and instilling in them a passion for knowledge.

To navigate the demanding nature of the teaching profession, it is important for educators to prioritize self-care, seek support from colleagues and mentors, and advocate for the well-being of themselves and their students. By fostering a culture of empathy, resilience, and continuous growth, educators can reignite their passion for teaching and contribute to the noble cause of shaping the future.

The road ahead will be challenging, but the potential for positive impact remains immeasurable. The perseverance of dedicated teachers is an invaluable asset in shaping the future, and we must do all we can to support and recognize their contributions to the betterment of society.

When I was in elementary school, I had epilepsy. As a young student struggling with factors outside of my control, I faced numerous challenges during my elementary school years, including frequent absences, intense brain testing, seizures, and the harsh side effects of strong medications. Despite the many obstacles I encountered, my story is defined by the unwavering support of my parents and an incredible group of educators who transformed what could have been a devastating period of my life into an unforgettable school experience.

Throughout those difficult times, my academic struggles and health concerns did not go unnoticed. My teachers played a pivotal role in shaping my perspective and strengthening my resolve. One educator in particular stands out as a beacon of compassion and support–Mrs. Boernke, my second-grade teacher.

The impact of Mrs. Boernke went far beyond the classroom; she transcended the traditional roles of a teacher, demonstrating an unparalleled commitment to her students. She recognized the unique challenges I faced and went above and beyond to support me, even checking on my well-being with a phone call in the middle of the night when I needed to stay up all night for special medical testing. Her kindness and compassion instilled in me a sense of resilience and a belief in my own potential.

Mrs. Boernke's legacy lives on through the enduring impact she had on my life. She was more than an educator; she was a role model of empathy and a testament to the power of believing in each student's potential. Her unwavering care and love motivated me to persevere in the face of my academic struggles and the emotional toll of managing a chronic condition. Her dedication to fostering mutual respect within the classroom created an environment where everyone felt valued and supported. It was evident that Mrs. Boernke saw me through God's eyes—caring about my whole well-being, not just my academic success, and seeing beyond my challenges.

> Don't hesitate to be enthusiastic—be on fire in
> the Spirit as you serve the Lord! (Romans 12:11)

Thanks to Mrs. Boernke and the exceptional educators who believed in me during those formative years, I developed a lasting appreciation for the importance of empathy, understanding, and the profound influence a teacher can have on a student's life. Mrs. Boernke's impact extended far beyond academic achievements. She inspired me to overcome challenges and become the educator and person I am today. Her actions will continue to resonate with me for years to come.

During my personal journey, I had an epiphany that drove my passion to become a teacher who would wholeheartedly embrace and support students who were facing greater challenges. I aimed to be the kind of educator who extended love to those whom may have been harder to connect with. This realization led me to pursue a career in special education, and over the course of fifteen years, I have traversed through various educational settings, accumulating diverse experiences that have enriched my understanding of the nuances within special education.

Currently serving as an instructional coach, I primarily support special education teachers, which allows me to witness a multitude of classrooms, each with its unique dynamics. However, one consistent observation that stands out to me is that when I remind myself of God's love for my students, the more readily patience and understanding flow from me. This recognition has become a cornerstone of my approach, influencing not only my interactions with students but also shaping the guidance that I provide to fellow educators.

Throughout my journey in special education, I have come to appreciate the significant impact of a caring and empathetic environment on students. My favorite moments are those when it's palpable that students feel genuinely cared for. Whenever I engage with teachers who prioritize creating such an atmosphere, they echo the sentiment that fostering a sense of care is their paramount objective.

Conversely, in my journey and specifically my role as a coach, I have come to an equally important realization, that teacher impatience often stems from a lack of understanding or a failure to maintain perspective. In the intricate tapestry of special education, where each student brings a unique set of challenges and strengths, it becomes crucial for educators to delve into the individual stories and perspectives that shape their students.

As an instructional coach, I have seen firsthand the transformative power of understanding and perspective. Teachers who comprehend their students' struggles, backgrounds, and learning styles are better equipped to navigate the complexities of special education and even general education. Whenever teachers lose patience, it is often a signal to revisit the foundation of understanding and perspective. Reconnecting with the stories that shape each student allows educators to respond with empathy, fostering an environment where patience and support become the guiding principles. The foundation of understanding these students is to remember that they are God's children. God loves them no matter what. This is always where we should start when trying to understand their stories. No matter how difficult their needs may be, no matter what their background, God loves them and then we can move forward from there.

In essence, my journey in special education has been a profound exploration of compassion, understanding, and intentional reflection on the divine love that serves as the bedrock of my approach. As I continue to support and guide special education teachers, my commitment to fostering environments where students feel cared for remains unwavering, knowing that it is through love, understanding, and perspective that the true essence of education unfolds. I am deeply passionate about my work, and I aim to make a difference in the lives of those students who need it most.

Navigating the intricate landscape of education can often leave teachers feeling bogged down by external pressures. Whether it's dealing with district policies, administrative changes, or external expectations, it's easy for educators to feel overwhelmed by factors that are beyond their control. This can result in heightened stress levels and a sense of diminished self-efficacy. The enormity of these external factors can leave teachers feeling powerless and frustrated, making it challenging for them to provide the best possible learning experience for their students.

However, a transformative shift occurs when teachers redirect their focus to what is within their sphere of influence. Recognizing and concentrating on aspects that are within their control empowers educators to make a more immediate and meaningful impact on both their students and their own mental well-being. By honing in on the microcosm of their classroom, teachers can cultivate a sense of agency and efficacy, which enhances the learning journey for students.

To achieve this, teachers need to embrace what is within their control while recognizing the profound impact of seeing students through the lens of compassion and understanding, as one might envision God's eyes. This involves refining instructional strategies, fostering positive classroom environments, establishing effective communication with students, and tailoring lessons to meet individual needs. By incorporating a perspective that acknowledges the inherent value and unique qualities each student possesses, teachers can create a transformative educational experience. This shift in focus not only facilitates a more positive and productive teaching experience but also enhances the learning journey for students, guided by a deeper sense of empathy and appreciation for each individual as seen through the eyes of God.

Concentrating on the controllable aspects of teaching also allows educators to navigate challenges with resilience. Instead of feeling overwhelmed by external pressures, we can focus on kingdom matters. Are our students feeling loved, respected? We can't solve every problem, so we should channel our energy into areas where we can genuinely make a difference.

This could be a place to bring up humans' basic needs and how those need to be met before a student can learn. By seeing students through God's eyes, we focus on those basic needs first before trying to provide them with new learning.

In essence, recognizing and prioritizing what is within one's control creates a more sustainable and fulfilling teaching experience. It is a paradigm that not only enhances the effectiveness of classroom instruction but also safeguards teachers' mental and emotional well-being in the face of external uncertainties. This shift in focus empowers educators to make a positive impact on their students and themselves and ultimately helps create a more supportive and successful learning environment for all.

Reflective Questions

How does the emphasis on prayer and reliance on God's guidance resonate with your own beliefs or experiences navigating challenges?

_____

_____

How do you perceive the role of a teacher in shaping not only academic skills but also life skills, values, and a love for learning?

_____

_____

Reflect on your own educational journey. Are there specific moments or experiences that have influenced your approach to teaching or your perspective on education?

_____

_____

CHAPTER 2

SEEING STUDENTS THROUGH GOD'S EYES

In the field of education, educators play a crucial role in shaping not only the academic dimension but also the emotional and social aspects of the learning environment. Guided by Christian values and inspired by their faith, teachers have the power to create a nurturing and supportive atmosphere that allows students to excel academically and grow personally.

A teacher's expression of love and appreciation for each student transcends conventional educational roles, reaching to the very core of personal development. By embracing the unique qualities and potential of each student, educators contribute to a supportive environment where students feel valued and understood within the context of their Christian faith.

Teachers can weave faith into their expressions of love and appreciation through personalized recognition by taking the time to understand the strengths, interests, and challenges of each student. Drawing inspiration from Christian principles of compassion, a teacher might publicly acknowledge a student's achievements, be they academic accomplishments, acts of kindness, or personal growth milestones. This recognition elevates the student's confidence and serves as a testimony to the entire class that each individual is seen and celebrated for their unique contributions.

Positive reinforcement techniques, infused with Christian encouragement, become a powerful tool in shaping a student's self-esteem and motivation. Educators can provide specific feedback on well-executed projects, emphasizing the student's effort, creativity, or improvement. This form of positive reinforcement communicates the teacher's commitment to the student's success, reflecting the Christian principle of supporting one another on their journey.

Building positive relationships, informed by Christian values of love and compassion, becomes a cornerstone of our words and actions. Taking the time to connect with students on a personal level and demonstrating genuine interest in their lives, concerns, and aspirations fosters a sense of trust and belonging. Engaging in casual conversations, participating in extracurricular activities, and understanding the cultural backgrounds and experiences of their students signifies that each student is an individual with unique stories and perspectives, worthy of attention and respect within the framework of Christian love.

Furthermore, teachers can actively contribute to an inclusive classroom environment that celebrates the beauty in our differences as a reflection of God's creation. Recognizing and appreciating the differences among students, whether cultural, linguistic, or ability-related, conveys a powerful message of acceptance. Integrating diverse perspectives into the curriculum, showcasing the achievements of individuals from various backgrounds, and encouraging students to share their unique experiences all align with the inclusive nature of Christian love.

The expression of love and appreciation by teachers within the Christian framework contributes to a positive and supportive educational environment. Here, students are not passive recipients of knowledge but active participants in their own growth, influenced by Christian principles of love, compassion, and acceptance. This approach creates a ripple effect, impacting not only academic outcomes but also shaping the character and well-being of students, inspiring them to engage in the learning process and develop the confidence to explore their God-given potential to the fullest. Overall, teachers have a pivotal role in shaping the academic, emotional, and social dimensions of the learning environment, guided by their faith and grounded in Christian principles.

Inherent Value and Dignity

Educators in the sanctity of the classroom are entrusted with a crucial responsibility that extends beyond imparting academic knowledge. They are also tasked with instilling in their students profound values that reflect the principles of dignity, respect, and kindness, all of which are rooted in the Christian belief that every individual possesses inherent worth. The cornerstone of fostering a positive and inclusive culture within the educational environment is teaching students about the intrinsic value of each person.

Promoting a culture of respect, kindness, and understanding is not only an ideal but also a practical application of Christian principles. Educators encourage students to recognize and celebrate the diversity of their classmates, providing a powerful framework for cultivating such a culture. In doing so, they inspire an atmosphere where differences are acknowledged and celebrated as reflections of God's intricate design, emphasizing that every student is a unique creation purposefully and intentionally made by God.

> For you created my inmost being; you knit me together in my mother's womb. I praise you because I am fearfully and wonderfully made; your works are wonderful, I know that full well. (Psalm 139:13–14)

Acknowledging diversity entails recognizing that students who appear different can often feel isolated, overlooked, or unloved. Therefore, it is vital to remind students of a fundamental Christian truth—that God created all human beings in His own image. This universal truth underscores the intrinsic worth and significance of every individual, irrespective of their differences or challenges. Reinforcing this belief helps educators cultivate an environment that counters exclusionary tendencies, fostering a sense of belonging for all students.

In challenging classroom situations, whether academic, social, or emotional, the Christian principle of love and acceptance becomes crucial. Emphasizing that each person, regardless of their unique characteristics or challenges, is created with purpose and significance serves as a reminder that everyone has a role in the grand tapestry of God's creation. By emphasizing this individuality, educators not only guide students to appreciate the beauty in diversity, recognizing that each individual contributes to the richness and depth of the collective learning experience, but we also remind ourselves.

This inclusive perspective extends beyond the academic realm, permeating the social dynamics of the classroom. When students understand their peers' inherent value, they are more likely to extend kindness, offer support, and build meaningful connections. In this atmosphere, the seeds of empathy are sown, allowing students to grasp the essence of Christian teachings that call for compassion and love for one another.

Growing up, we had one distinguishable student who had a disability. He had a hard time controlling his emotions and often had a support person with him. I am not sure what disability he had, but I know that he struggled academically, socially, and behaviorally. We weren't told much about his struggles, and he was ostracized from groups. He was always picked last for teams, and no one played with him at recess. Looking back, I wonder how the staff could have taught us about how to best include him and recognize his strengths.

On the other hand, there was another memorable experience a few years later that demonstrated the power of acceptance and compassion. We had a couple of students who were struggling socially and didn't have any friends. Our teacher took time to spotlight our strengths in class. We learned more about our classmates, and our teacher taught us how to understand disabilities as a whole and how to have compassion for those who are struggling. She started implementing activities that played on different strengths, allowing us to appreciate one another and see the struggling students in a more positive light.

By instilling the understanding that God created all in His own image, educators lay the groundwork for a compassionate and inclusive society where each person is recognized, celebrated, and loved for their unique qualities and contributions. Ultimately, this outlook will prepare students to be compassionate leaders, influencers, and global citizens who embody Christian principles and strive to create a more equitable and inclusive world.

> So God created human beings in His own image. In the image of God he created them; male and female he created them. (Genesis 1:27)

As educators, guiding students to explore their unique talents, interests, and aspirations is a profound undertaking that extends far beyond the confines of traditional classroom boundaries. Creating an environment that celebrates individuality empowers students to recognize the distinct gifts they bring to the table, enriching the learning experience. Below are examples of this:

- In physical education classes, provide opportunities for students to choose fitness activities that align with their interests and personal goals. This could include options such as yoga, team sports, or individual fitness challenges. Celebrating progress and improvement rather than enforcing a one-size-fits-all approach encourages a lifelong commitment to physical well-being. This can change years of dread and humiliation to feelings of achievement and allows students to enjoy their physical education classes even if they don't fit into the "popular" stereotype.
- Provide students with choices for literature assignments. Allowing them to pick books that resonate with their interests fosters a love for reading and literature. One student might be drawn to classic novels, while another may find inspiration in contemporary poetry.
- Encourage students to pursue projects that align with their personal interests. For instance, a student

fascinated by astronomy might delve into a self-directed research project on a celestial phenomenon, fostering a love for STEM subjects and motivating deeper learning.

Encouraging students to delve into their talents involves providing opportunities for self-discovery through interactive projects, creative assignments, and extracurricular activities that showcase their unique abilities. By doing so, educators not only nurture individual growth but also cultivate an atmosphere where students appreciate the diverse skills and talents of their peers.

Furthermore, guiding students to understand that they are part of a larger plan taps into the biblical principle of purpose and divine design. Helping them see the interconnectedness of their individual journeys within the broader context of the classroom, school, and world instills a sense of responsibility and significance. It communicates the idea that each student plays a vital role in the collective tapestry of God's plan.

Setting goals becomes a natural progression in this process of self-discovery and purpose. Educators can guide students in articulating both short-term and long-term goals by aligning them with their talents and aspirations. This practice cultivates a sense of direction and purposeful living, along with a sense of ownership over one's education. Students begin to understand that their goals are not isolated pursuits but integral components of their larger purpose in contributing positively to the world around them.

In the Christian context, the idea of contributing positively embodies the principles of love, service, and stewardship. Educators can encourage students to reflect on how their unique talents can be employed for the betterment of their communities, fostering a spirit of empathy and social responsibility. This aligns with Christian teachings that emphasize the importance of using one's gifts to positively impact others.

Guiding students toward a hopeful future encompasses more than just academic success. It involves instilling in them a resilience that transcends challenges and setbacks. Educators can draw on Christian principles of faith and hope, encouraging students to face obstacles with a steadfast spirit, trusting that their unique gifts and purposes are part of a greater plan.

Ultimately, the process of helping students explore their talents, interests, and aspirations within a Christian framework is a transformative journey. It not only shapes the trajectory of individual lives but contributes to the creation of a compassionate and purpose-driven community. By weaving these principles into the fabric of education, educators play a vital role in nurturing individuals who understand and embrace their unique place in the divine plan, creating a better future for all.

> For I know the plans I have for you, declares
> the Lord, plans for welfare and not for evil, to
> give you a future and a hope. (Jeremiah 29:11)

You may say, "That all sounds great, Alyssa, but you haven't met my students. How am I supposed to be intentional with doing all that when I'm juggling so much?" Here's the answer: this is a mindset change; the actions naturally come with it. Much like when you first gave your heart to God—you changed your heart and mind and, eventually, your actions started to follow along.

My kids are learning the "Fruit of the Spirit" song at church. When I say they're learning it, I mean they think they should be singing it a million times a day. Don't get me wrong, it's much better than hearing "Baby Shark" all day. I started asking them if they knew what each fruit of the Spirit meant, and they had a hard time coming up with an explanation for them. Diving into the fruits of the Spirit is a great, tangible way to explore how to start seeing changes in both your heart and actions.

> But the fruit of the Spirit is love, joy, peace, forbearance, kindness, goodness, faithfulness, gentleness, and self-control. Against such things, there is no law. (Galatians 5:22–23)

Love weaves its way intricately into the role of a teacher, not only shaping the educational experience but the very essence of human connection within the learning community. To genuinely care for and connect with students, it is essential to recognize their unique needs and aspirations. This involves active listening, providing support, and showing sincere interest in their well-being. Love extends beyond the students themselves, reaching coworkers and parents, and fostering a collaborative and supportive environment. By cultivating a positive and inclusive classroom, educators create a space where each student feels valued and accepted, celebrating diversity and ensuring that every voice is heard. Empathy and understanding are the foundations of love in action, allowing teachers to connect with their students on a deeper level and respond to their individual challenges with compassion. In essence, love in education is a transformative force that not only nurtures academic growth but also emotional and social development for each member of the learning community.

As educators, we have the power to transform our classrooms into spaces where students thrive both academically and emotionally. Joy, one of the fruits of the Spirit, becomes a guiding force in our educational journey, shaping not only the content but also the very spirit of our teaching. By infusing enthusiasm and passion into the classroom, we create an environment where learning becomes a joyful exploration. This fervor extends to celebrating achievements and milestones, big and small, fostering a culture where every success, whether academic or personal, is acknowledged and cherished. This creates an atmosphere infused with positivity, inspiring and motivating our students to engage with the learning process.

Another essential virtue, peace, transforms our classrooms into havens of tranquility. By maintaining a calm and composed demeanor in challenging situations, we set the tone for constructive problem-solving. By promoting conflict resolution and nurturing a harmonious and respectful culture, we create a space where students feel secure and supported.

Patience, or forbearance, is a virtue that shapes the teacher-student relationship. Navigating through student challenges and learning curves with patience demonstrates an understanding that growth takes time. This patience extends to interactions with parents and coworkers, fostering an atmosphere of collaboration and mutual support. How do you stay patient in the midst of utter chaos? It's different for everyone. I myself like a good deep breath and a quick prayer as I battle the everyday chaos. I also think it's important to find other believers you can go to in your time of need. That way when you're about to lose your cool, you can vent and pray with someone who will guide you in the right way.

Kindness, as a manifestation of love, finds expression in daily actions. Practicing random acts of kindness within the classroom and the broader school community creates a ripple effect of positivity. Offering encouraging words becomes a simple yet impactful way to uplift students, parents, and colleagues, creating a culture where kindness is intentional and pervasive.

Goodness, rooted in moral integrity and ethical behavior, forms the foundation of a virtuous educational environment. Modeling positive character traits for students becomes a guiding principle, reinforcing the importance of ethical conduct. Contributing to a school environment that upholds values of goodness creates a culture where integrity is cherished and upheld.

Faithfulness, beyond reliability, encompasses a commitment to professional ethics and standards. By building trust through consistent actions and words, we create an environment where students, parents, and colleagues feel secure and supported.

Faithful educators prioritize transparency in their interactions with students, parents, and colleagues. They communicate openly about classroom expectations, learning objectives, and student progress. This fosters confidence and reinforces a sense of security within the educational community, ensuring that everyone is aligned regarding the educational journey.

Integrity is an essential cornerstone of faithfulness. Educators who uphold high moral and ethical standards are regarded with admiration and inspire confidence from their peers, students, and parents. Educational integrity encompasses fair grading, unbiased assessment methods, and an unwavering commitment to honesty. By modeling integrity, faithful educators instill these values in their students, contributing to the development of responsible and ethical individuals.

Gentleness in teaching is a transformative force that shapes the approach to challenges and conflicts. By approaching difficulties with a gentle and understanding spirit, we create an atmosphere where mistakes are seen as opportunities for growth. Providing constructive feedback with kindness and tact becomes a hallmark of teaching, fostering a nurturing environment. These kids don't need to be yelled at, they need to be redirected with gentleness and forgiveness. Many of our students are getting yelled at by their parents, and when we try to redirect a student in anger, the student simply shuts down and does not hear what we are telling them. If we approach a conflict with gentleness, however, the student will let their guard down, become more vulnerable, and change may be able to take place.

Finally, self-control is a virtue that guides us through the complexities of the profession. Exhibiting self-discipline and control in stressful situations models healthy coping mechanisms for students. Demonstrating balanced decision-making and emotional regulation creates a classroom environment where both teachers and students thrive. Self-control is also vital when communicating with other adults. We can fall into the patterns of the world if we are working with those with different values and beliefs than us. In wanting to fit in, we may say things that are not Christ-like. We need to monitor our thoughts and words so that they are a reflection of God's light through us.

> Those who guard their mouths and their tongues keep themselves from calamity. (Proverbs 21:23)

In essence, embodying these fruits not only enriches the educational experience but also contributes to the holistic development of our students and the creation of a positive and uplifting learning community. As educators, we have the opportunity to create an environment that nurtures the mind, body, and spirit of our students.

Did you know that you were created with a divine purpose? That's right; you were specifically crafted by God for God. You are here for a reason. Have you taken a moment to ask Him what that reason is? Have you prayed for Him to work through you to help your students reach their purpose?

Ephesians 2:10 (NIV) says, "For we are God's handiwork, created in Christ Jesus to do good works, which God prepared in advance for us to do."

Let's break this verse down to explore how it applies to the school system.

God's Handiwork

The term "handiwork" in this verse speaks to the depth of God's investment in us. He has invested in a personal relationship with us, constantly yearning to be close and connected with His creation. This all-knowing, all-powerful Creator, who spoke the world into existence, considers you His handiwork. We don't use the term handiwork for things that we simply throw together without much thought or effort; we use this term when we meticulously plan every aspect and painstakingly work at creating something that we are proud of. God is proud of you. He created each one of us uniquely, paying close attention to every detail. He crafted each person, including you, your family, and your students, with distinct talents, skills, and potential.

Created in Christ Jesus

As believers, our true identity is found in Christ. Everything we do, say, and think should be a reflection of His love for us. As educators, it is vital that we remember our students were also created for Him. We must ensure that all we do, say, and even think is an accurate representation of Christ's love and not just a reflection of worldly values. While you're teaching, ensure you are putting Christ's love into action by doing, saying, and thinking it for your students.

To Do Good Works

We are called to do good works in the name of God's love. By exemplifying this behavior, we can instill strong morals and values in our students, contributing to the creation of a better community. For instance, by organizing community service projects or promoting acts of kindness within the school, we actively contribute to the betterment of our community. However, doing good works does not mean we must be pushovers and say yes to every request. Instead, we must utilize the wisdom that God has given us to help others.

Prepared in Advance

Let's just pause here for a second. Isn't it great to know that God has prepared this all for us in advance? He has prepared for us to do good works in his name. He has a plan for us (Jeremiah 29:11). This also means that God knew of the hardships we would face long before we were born. If you are feeling burnt out or frustrated, if you are struggling with a particular student or coworker, know that God prepared you for this very moment. He has given you the heart and gifts needed to make an impact on the exact individuals you were meant to serve. Though we may not always end up where we thought we would, we end up exactly where God placed us, and He prepares us for these moments in advance.

A few years ago, my husband was cut from his teaching job due to boundary changes. He was looking for jobs and eventually got hired for a part-time teaching position at an elementary school. He was hoping to find another teaching position that would total up to him being full time again but ended up subbing to compensate for being part time. It was stressful financially for us, but we made it work. He finally found another teaching job in our district to add up to make him full time, just in time for schools to shut down due to the COVID-19 pandemic. We were in awe of the timing because it allowed him to get a full paycheck. If he had still been subbing, he wouldn't have gotten paid for that while schools were shut down. It was *so* obvious to us that God was making Himself known to us by reminding us that His providence presides over all and that we need to trust Him no matter what.

So as you head into your classroom or office, remember that you were created with a divine purpose. Embrace the fact that you are God's handiwork and know that He has equipped you to make a positive impact in the lives of your students.

Every child has a different learning style and pace. Each child is unique, not only capable of learning but also capable of succeeding.
—Robert John Meehan

Reflective Questions

Reflect on how the fruits of the Spirit (love, joy, peace, forbearance, kindness, goodness, faithfulness, gentleness, and self-control) manifest in your teaching. Are there areas where you can intentionally cultivate these virtues for both you and your students?

_____

_____

Reflect on Ephesians 2:10 and how it applies to your role as an educator. How does recognizing that you are God's handiwork influence your perspective on your purpose and impact in the classroom?

_____

_____

How do you utilize wisdom, guided by Christian principles, in deciding what decisions you're going to make, especially when faced with multiple demands and challenges in your role as an educator?

_____

_____

CHAPTER 3

APPLYING CHRIST'S
TEACHINGS IN THE SCHOOL

As you read, you may notice that I don't directly discuss educating students about faith. Unfortunately, for many of us, we work in settings that prohibit such conversations. It's frustrating because the public school system places constraints on us, making it feel like a constant battle. The ever-present constraints imposed by the public school system add an extra layer of complexity to an educator's mission. The policies and norms can make discussing faith a daunting task, causing teachers to proceed with caution. Crossing the established boundaries can result in severe consequences, including termination. The stakes are high, making it all the more imperative for educators to remain mindful of the constraints and tread carefully.

We want to maintain our personal integrity and stay true to our beliefs, but we have to navigate conversations with precision to avoid the appearance of proselytizing or advocating for a particular faith. The battle to adhere to these constraints while maintaining personal integrity and staying true to one's beliefs is nothing short of exhausting.

However, for those fortunate educators who have the freedom to engage in open discussions about faith, I'm thrilled for you and your students. Even if you don't face the same restrictions, the strategies outlined here are valuable for all educators. It's essential to maintain professionalism while also fostering a respectful and inclusive learning environment.

Teaching in the public realm, where institutional views and policies may conflict with personal beliefs, requires a delicate and strategic approach. It involves a nuanced understanding of when to stand firm and when to navigate the terrain more cautiously. One key aspect of this navigation is identifying the proverbial "hill you're willing to die on." In other words, determining the issues or principles so crucial to your convictions that you would be prepared to face professional consequences, including possible litigation and/or termination, for upholding them. Here are five essential tips to keep in mind when navigating teaching in a school system that may not align with your values and beliefs as a Christian.

1. Define Your Core Values

Clearly defining your core values is the foundational step in navigating the intersection of personal beliefs and institutional policies. As a Christian educator, this involves identifying the principles rooted in your faith that guide your actions and decisions. These may include values such as compassion, empathy, and commitment to fostering a positive and inclusive learning environment.

2. Evaluate Professional Risks

There may be a time when you are asked to teach something that you don't agree with. Beyond understanding the potential risks, it's essential to assess the practical implications of standing firm on certain issues. Consider the possible consequences, both professionally and personally, and weigh them against the importance of maintaining your convictions. This evaluation requires a realistic understanding of the institutional climate and the potential impact on your career.

3. Seek Common Ground

Look for areas where your Christian values intersect with broader educational goals and values. Emphasize those commonalities to create bridges of understanding with colleagues, administrators, and even students. By highlighting shared objectives, you can foster a collaborative environment that respects diverse perspectives.

4. Engage in Constructive Dialogue

Constructive dialogue is a powerful tool for fostering understanding and mitigating conflicts. Approach conversations with colleagues and administrators with a willingness to listen and learn from different perspectives. By expressing your views in a respectful and open manner, you create an environment that encourages reciprocal understanding.

5. Know Your Legal Rights

Being aware of your legal rights as a Christian educator is crucial. Familiarize yourself with the laws governing religious freedom and expression in educational settings. This knowledge provides a solid foundation for advocating for your rights within the legal boundaries, ensuring that you can navigate challenges with clarity and confidence. There are various Christian organizations that will help you if you have a legal need, such as Christian Educators or Alliance Defending Freedom.[2]

In the intricate dance of personal faith and professional obligations, these considerations serve as guidelines. By defining your core values, assessing risks, seeking common ground, engaging in constructive dialogue, and understanding your legal rights, you equip yourself to navigate the complexities of teaching within a school system that may not fully align with your Christian values. Through thoughtful and strategic actions, you can uphold your convictions while contributing positively to the educational environment.

Incorporating the principles of patience, forgiveness, and genuine acceptance into your interactions with others is crucial when embodying Christ's love in a public school setting. Keep in mind the difference between acceptance and approval. We can accept and love our students without approving of their choices and lifestyles. We must model our actions after Jesus. He came down to earth and spent time with people who did not agree with Him. Instead of conforming to their ways, He showed them love and mercy. Demonstrating these qualities requires conscious effort, but doing so can make a profound impact on the school community. Here are some practical ways to demonstrate Christ's love in a public school.

We can accept and love our students without approving of their choices and lifestyles.

---

[2] See the list of resources at the back of the book for more information.

Patience

To demonstrate patience, create an environment where differences are respected and embraced. Be tolerant of diverse perspectives and opinions, as people in a school setting come from various backgrounds, cultures, and experiences. Understanding the challenges that students may be facing, both academically and personally, can create a compassionate and supportive atmosphere that reflects Christ's patience and understanding. Let us remember that every student is a unique creation with their own strengths, struggles, and stories. Just as Christ saw individuals beyond their immediate circumstances, we, too, can strive to look beyond surface differences and acknowledge the inherent dignity within each person. By exercising patience, we not only model Christ's teachings but also contribute to the richness and vibrancy of the educational tapestry we create together.

Forgiveness

Forgiveness should be promoted and encouraged among students and colleagues, as everyone makes mistakes. Acknowledging this fact and emphasizing the importance of learning and growing from those experiences can create a culture of forgiveness. Modeling forgiveness in conflicts is essential, as Christ's forgiveness serves as a powerful example, contributing to a harmonious school environment.

Spending Time with Others

Taking the time to build meaningful relationships with students, teachers, and staff is a way of demonstrating Christ's love. Christ spent time with sinners, demonstrating the value of personal connections, and being genuinely interested in others' lives, challenges, and triumphs can create an atmosphere of acceptance. Offering your time and support to those who may be struggling, just as Christ invested in the lives of others, can make a lasting impact.

Encourage Personal Growth

When accepting people as they are, it is essential to encourage personal growth and development. Christ accepted individuals but also inspired them to become better versions of themselves, and supporting others in their journey of self-improvement can make a difference. In the spirit of this transformative approach, let us be not only accepting but also catalysts for positive change. Just as a gardener tends to a plant, providing the right conditions for it to grow, we, too, can nurture the potential within each person, fostering an environment where seeds of self-improvement blossom into the flowers of personal success. As educators, we hold the power to cultivate not just academic achievement but also the character and resilience that will carry our students through life's challenges. Let our support be the gentle rain that waters the aspirations of those around us, helping them bloom into the fullness of their God-given potential.

Service and Compassion

Acts of kindness and service can demonstrate Christ's love. Volunteering your time to help others, whether it's assisting with school events, tutoring, or participating in community service projects, can make a positive impact. Showing empathy and compassion, especially toward those who may be vulnerable or marginalized, can embody Christ's teachings.

Incorporating these principles into your daily interactions and involvement in the school community can effectively demonstrate Christ's love in a public school setting. By making love, patience, forgiveness, and acceptance central values, you can contribute to a positive and uplifting atmosphere. Remember, small actions can make a big difference in the lives of those around you.

> Whatever you do, work at it with all your heart, as working for the Lord, not for human masters, since you know that you will receive an inheritance from the Lord as a reward. It is the Lord Christ you are serving. (Colossians 3:23–24)

As you reflect on your mindset going into your classroom, which students push your buttons more than the others? Is there a specific group or groups of students that just push your buttons more than others? Odds are those students are challenging for more than just you. They may be pushed aside or forgotten about because they're not in the majority. How can you be intentional about showing those students that you want them to be a part of the learning community? Here are some practical strategies that may help engage those students that may need more attention:

- Learn about your students at a personal level.[3] Many times, those students that we have more difficulty with have so much more going on than meets the eye. Get to know what they like and dislike. Ask them about their favorite TV show or how their basketball team did last night. Sometimes students just need time to trust you.

---

[3] See the resources section for some great activities for this.

- Focus on the positives, and encourage them. Encourage your students when you see them doing something positive. Look to see what makes them light up. Does it make them feel like a million bucks to get a positive note from you? Be specific in your praise, pointing out exactly what the student did well. Acknowledge the effort students put into their work, and celebrate improvements they make over time. Our goal is to positively encourage students while building autonomy.

- Acknowledge the difficulty you are both having. Kids are so much smarter than we give them credit for. They know when something is difficult for you and often will lose trust if you lie and just tell them everything is great when it's really not. Be honest about what the challenge is. Here's a frame for doing this: "When you _____ it makes me feel _____. What can we do instead?"

For example, "When you yell in class, it's disruptive to everyone, and it makes me feel frustrated. What can we do instead of yelling when you want my attention?"

Reflective Questions

How do the described challenges of navigating conversations about faith in a public school setting resonate with your own experiences?

_____

_____

What "hills are you willing to die on" in terms of upholding your convictions in an educational setting?

_____

_____

How do you currently incorporate principles of patience, forgiveness, and acceptance into your interactions with students and colleagues?

_____

_____

CHAPTER 4

GETTING TO KNOW THE
HEARTS OF YOUR STUDENTS

Mr. Thompson, a dedicated sixth-grade teacher at Monroe Elementary, was faced with the daily challenges of managing a diverse classroom. Among his students was Jake, a bright and enthusiastic boy who, despite his intelligence, struggled with outbursts that disrupted the class. Initially frustrated by Jake's frequent disruptions, Mr. Thompson found himself repeatedly telling the young boy to stop. He could see the confusion and frustration in Jake's eyes after each outburst, but the cycle seemed unbreakable.

Determined to find a solution, Mr. Thompson decided to seek guidance from the school's special education teacher Mrs. Rodriguez. During their conversation, Mrs. Rodriguez shared valuable insights about Jake's individual needs. She explained that Jake, who had autism, might be experiencing sensory overload, which would contribute to his outbursts. With this new information, Mr. Thompson felt a renewed sense of empathy and understanding toward Jake.

Mr. Thompson and Mrs. Rodriguez decided to work together to create a supportive environment for Jake. They transformed a corner of the classroom into a calming space, complete with soft lighting, comfortable cushions, and noise-canceling headphones. The idea was to provide Jake with a sanctuary where he could retreat whenever he felt overwhelmed.

One day during a particularly challenging lesson, Jake's frustration reached a breaking point. Instead of reprimanding him, Mr. Thompson approached with a gentler tone. "Hey, Jake," he said, crouching down beside him. "I noticed things are tough right now. How about we use our calming space for a bit? It's here for you whenever you need it."

Surprised by the understanding tone, Jake hesitated but eventually nodded. As he settled into the calming space, the soothing ambiance began to work its magic. The other students continued with their tasks, and the classroom maintained its rhythm. Over time, Mr. Thompson became attuned to Jake's cues, proactively suggesting breaks in the calming space before outbursts occurred.

The once-disruptive episodes began to wane, and a sense of harmony settled over the classroom. The positive change in Jake's behavior did not go unnoticed by his classmates. Slowly, they began to understand and accept the importance of the calming space. In turn, the classroom transformed into a supportive community where everyone felt valued.

Reflecting on the transformative journey he and Jake had taken together, Mr. Thompson was filled with pride as he watched Jake confidently walk across the stage during the graduation ceremony. The once-frustrating outbursts were replaced with a sense of accomplishment and belonging. This powerful story of Jake's journey became a reminder that a little understanding, compassion, and collaborative effort can transform challenges into opportunities for growth and connection.

Sometimes when we are having a hard time looking at someone in a positive light, it's due to a lack of understanding. If we take a moment in the frustration to just breathe and remind ourselves that they are a child of God, it can help us get into the mindset of seeing them as a person instead of just a challenge. If a student has a disability, we may not understand how that truly can affect them—cognitively, behaviorally, and socially. If a student has a history of trauma, we don't always make the connections to their behavior.

> For the Lord gives wisdom; from his mouth
> come knowledge and understanding.
> (Proverbs 2:6)

Students with Disabilities

There are multiple disabilities that affect our students, and I will always recommend learning about the specific disabilities that affect your students and how they are affected. Here are some of the impacts and teaching strategies for autism, attention deficit hyperactivity disorder (ADHD), emotional and behavioral disorders (EBD), and students dealing with trauma, which are some of the most commonly misunderstood disabilities.

1. Autism Spectrum Disorder (ASD)

ASD is a complex neurodevelopmental disorder that impacts cognitive, behavioral, and social functioning. Students with ASD require a specialized approach to learning that considers the unique challenges they face and the individual strengths they possess. By learning more about your students with autism, you are able to reach them where they are at and build upon their strengths. These are just some of the impacts you may see in your students with autism.

Behavioral Impact

Repetitive behaviors are a common symptom of ASD, including hand flapping or rocking. While these behaviors may appear odd to some, they often serve as self-regulatory mechanisms. By recognizing and validating these behaviors and then working collaboratively with the student to identify alternative strategies for self-regulation, educators can create a supportive environment that fosters academic and social success, as well as protect the student.

Changes in routine or unexpected transitions can be challenging for individuals with ASD. Visual schedules and advanced notice of changes can help students prepare and minimize anxiety, leading to a more stable and comfortable learning environment. Consistency in routines is also important for promoting success. To increase success with transitions, other strategies to try are timers, choices, first/then schedules, providing advanced warning, and using transition objects.

Cognitive Impact

Individuals with ASD often exhibit differences in cognitive processing styles that require tailored instruction. These differences may include difficulties with language processing and social cues but could include strengths in other areas, such as mathematics and memorization. By identifying these differences, educators can create instructional methods that cater to individual strengths and challenges.

Many individuals with ASD experience sensory sensitivities that impact their cognitive processing abilities. Bright lights, loud noises, or certain textures may be overwhelming, making it difficult for students to learn and engage with others. Creating a sensory-friendly environment that incorporates natural lighting and noise-canceling headphones can significantly enhance cognitive functioning for these students and even neurotypical students.

Social Impact

Many individuals with ASD experience difficulties in social communication, including difficulties with nonverbal cues and reciprocal conversations. Implementing social skills training and structured peer interactions can promote social development.

Socializing and forming friendships can be challenging for students with ASD. To promote positive relationships and understanding among classmates, educators can assign peer buddies, create inclusive activities, and implement peer education programs.

Sensory sensitivities may lead to social withdrawal or avoidance of certain social situations. Creating sensory-friendly spaces or providing sensory breaks can help students with ASD participate more comfortably in social activities.

Teaching Strategies and Considerations

Teaching students with autism requires an approach that considers their individual cognitive processing styles. One effective strategy is to tailor instruction based on each student's strengths. For instance, incorporating mathematical concepts and patterns into other subjects can help enhance engagement and understanding.

Another crucial aspect is creating a sensory-friendly environment. This can be achieved by using natural lighting, noise-canceling headphones, and minimizing overwhelming stimuli. These measures can improve cognitive processing abilities and make the learning environment more comfortable for students.

Furthermore, managing transitions is vital in helping students with autism thrive in the classroom. Visual schedules and advance notice of changes can ease the stress associated with transitions. Consistent routines and clear communication about schedule alterations can also reduce anxiety and contribute to a stable learning environment.

Overall, using a holistic approach that addresses the individual needs of each student can help ensure that students with autism receive the support they require to reach their full potential. By implementing these teaching strategies, we can create an inclusive learning environment where every student can thrive.

Understanding the interplay between cognitive, behavioral, and social aspects is essential for developing effective strategies to support students with ASD. It's important to recognize that every person with ASD has a unique combination of strengths and challenges. By creating a supportive and inclusive learning environment, educators can help students with ASD thrive academically and socially while promoting understanding and acceptance among their peers. Ultimately, it's through our efforts to understand and support students with ASD that we can foster a more compassionate and inclusive society for all.

2. Attention Deficit Hyperactivity Disorder (ADHD)

ADHD is a neurodevelopmental disorder that affects both children and adults. It is a condition that can significantly impact various aspects of an individual's life, from their academic performance to their social interactions and cognitive functioning.[4]

Behavioral Impact

The behavioral impact of ADHD can manifest in different ways. Students with ADHD may find it challenging to sustain attention, making it difficult to focus on tasks, follow instructions, and complete assignments. Some students with ADHD may display hyperactive behaviors, such as fidgeting, restlessness, and difficulty staying seated for extended periods. Impulsivity can lead to challenges in decision-making and self-control. It can make students act without thinking about the consequences, leading to impulsive behaviors. Emotional regulation can also be challenging for students with ADHD. They may experience mood swings, frustration, and difficulty managing emotions.

---

[4] American Psychiatric Association, 2013

Cognitive Impact

ADHD often affects executive functions, such as working memory, cognitive flexibility, and organization. This can impact a student's ability to plan, prioritize, and complete tasks, affecting their cognitive functioning. Inconsistent attention and difficulty organizing tasks may lead to academic challenges. However, it's important to note that intelligence is not affected by ADHD, and many individuals with ADHD have average or above-average intelligence. Some students with ADHD may also have co-occurring learning disabilities, further complicating the academic challenges they face.

Social Impact

ADHD can also have a significant social impact. Students with ADHD may face difficulties forming and maintaining friendships due to impulsive behaviors or challenges in social cues. Social skills deficits are common, as students with ADHD may struggle with taking turns, listening, and understanding nonverbal communication. Academic and social challenges may contribute to lower self-esteem in students with ADHD, particularly if they face criticism or negative feedback from peers and teachers. The difficulties associated with ADHD can also contribute to feelings of anxiety and depression in some individuals.

Teaching Strategies and Considerations

Teaching students with ADHD requires a dynamic and empathetic approach that accounts for the unique challenges and needs of each individual learner. With this in mind, there are a range of effective strategies that can be employed in the classroom to support these students in achieving their full potential.

One crucial aspect of effective teaching for students with ADHD is the use of clear and consistent instructions. Providing instructions in a clear and concise manner, both verbally and visually (pictures or writing), can help to reduce confusion and provide structure. It can also be helpful to break down tasks into smaller, more manageable steps, using visual aids and lists to reinforce key points.

In addition to clear instructions, creating a structured environment can be incredibly beneficial for students with ADHD. This can involve establishing and maintaining a consistent daily routine, clearly defining rules and expectations, and using visual cues to help students anticipate transitions and activities. By providing a sense of predictability and order, this type of structure can help to create a more supportive and calming learning environment.

Another important aspect of effective teaching for students with ADHD is active engagement. This can involve incorporating hands-on and interactive learning activities, as well as encouraging movement breaks or short physical activities to help release excess energy. The use of technology, educational games, and multimedia resources can also be helpful in making lessons more engaging and interactive.

Recognizing that students with ADHD may have different learning styles is also crucial. Offering a variety of instructional methods, such as visual aids, auditory explanations, and hands-on activities, can help to accommodate these different styles and support learning. Additionally, allowing for flexible seating arrangements and providing frequent feedback can help to ensure that each student is able to learn and succeed to the best of their abilities.

Other key strategies for supporting students with ADHD in the classroom include time management techniques, organizational support, breaking tasks into manageable chunks, peer support, and positive reinforcement. By working collaboratively with parents, special education professionals, and other support staff, it is possible to create individualized plans that address the unique needs of each student with ADHD. With consistent communication and feedback, it is possible to continually tailor these strategies to best meet the evolving needs of each individual student.

In short, ADHD is a complex disorder that can impact multiple areas of an individual's life. By understanding the challenges associated with ADHD, we can better support and assist individuals with this condition. It's essential to approach ADHD with patience and compassion, recognizing that each person's experience with the disorder is unique. With proper support and resources, individuals with ADHD can thrive and achieve success in all areas of their lives.

3. Emotional Behavioral Disorders (EBD)

When it comes to students with EBD, there's a lot to consider. They're dealing with a range of challenges that impact their cognitive, behavioral, and social domains. As educators and peers, it's essential that we understand just how much these disorders can affect a student's ability to learn and grow.[5]

Behavioral Impact

The behavioral impact of EBD can be significant and far-reaching. One area of concern is disruptive behavior, which can manifest in a variety of ways, such as outbursts or defiance.

---

[5] American Psychiatric Association, 2013

These types of behaviors can seriously disrupt the learning environment and have a negative impact on the overall classroom atmosphere.

Cognitive Impact

Academic tasks can pose a real challenge for students who are experiencing emotional and behavioral difficulties. These students often have trouble with concentration, memory retention, and maintaining their attention span, which can seriously impact their academic performance. In some cases, students may resort to maladaptive coping mechanisms, such as avoiding tasks or engaging in disruptive behavior, which can only serve to make the situation worse by impeding their ability to fully engage with the learning process.

Social Impact

One of the many challenges that students with emotional and behavioral disorders face is difficulty understanding social cues. This struggle can lead to misinterpretations and cause difficulties in social interactions. It is important to note that this challenge may stem from their disability and not from a lack of interest or motivation to interact socially.

Another impact of EBD is that students may suffer from low self-esteem due to persistent behavioral challenges. This can have a detrimental effect on their overall well-being and can contribute to feelings of worthlessness and inadequacy.

Teaching Strategies and Considerations

By breaking down tasks into smaller, more manageable steps and providing clear instructions, you can help students feel less overwhelmed and more confident in their abilities. Offering additional support, such as one-on-one assistance or access to a resource room, can also go a long way in ensuring student success.

Moreover, incorporating inclusive activities that encourage positive social interactions and promote the building of a supportive peer network can make a significant difference in the classroom environment. It's also important to provide a designated space for self-regulation if needed so that students have a safe and calming space to retreat to when feeling overwhelmed.

Individuals with autism and other disabilities may exhibit atypical behaviors in response to high levels of stress. These actions are not intended to defy authority but rather an automatic response to perceived threats. Limited coping skills, communication challenges, and heightened sensory sensitivity can all contribute to such behaviors. In order to provide appropriate support, it is essential to recognize the unique needs of each student, understand their triggers, and approach the situation with empathy and a trauma-informed perspective. Collaboration with special education professionals and personalized interventions can promote an inclusive learning environment. Ultimately, compassion and targeted support are crucial for creating a positive educational experience for students with disabilities.

Students with a History of Trauma

Being mindful of the behavioral, academic, and social impacts of trauma can help educators better understand and support students who have experienced it. By creating a compassionate and supportive learning environment, we can help students feel safe, build trust, and ultimately thrive.

Behavioral Impact

Students who have experienced trauma may exhibit challenging behaviors as a way of coping. These behaviors, such as aggression or withdrawal, should be seen as protective responses rather than disruptions in the classroom. By understanding the student's history, educators can approach them with empathy and implement trauma-informed practices, such as creating a safe and predictable environment, to help them feel more secure.

Cognitive Impact

The impact of trauma on cognitive function can be significant, potentially leading to difficulties with memory and concentration. It is important for teachers to recognize the academic repercussions of trauma and provide additional support. This can include creating individualized learning plans and taking a supportive approach to help students navigate academic challenges stemming from their traumatic experiences. It's important for us to remember that if a student's basic needs are not being met, they will not be able to focus on school and learn. If they are not feeling safe, they are not going to be ready to learn.

Social Impact

Trauma can also impact a student's social well-being by affecting their ability to trust others and form healthy relationships. As educators, we can work toward building trusting relationships with our students and offer them avenues for counseling or support. Encouraging positive peer relationships and providing opportunities for students to express themselves can also contribute to their social well-being.

Teaching Strategies and Considerations

Creating a learning environment that supports students who have experienced trauma requires careful thought and planning. It's important to establish trust, develop individualized support plans, maintain routine and predictability, set clear expectations, incorporate trauma-informed practices, provide emotional support, and collaborate with support services.

One way to build trust and establish a safe environment is to start the school year with activities that foster a sense of community and encourage open communication. It's also important to recognize that trust may take time to develop and to provide a safe space for students to share their thoughts and feelings.

Establishing a predictable daily routine can also create a sense of safety for students who have experienced trauma. It's important to clearly communicate any changes in advance and provide visual schedules. When changes are unavoidable, it's helpful to provide reassurance and support to help students navigate the transition.

Setting clear expectations for behavior and academic performance can also foster a positive and supportive learning environment. Using positive reinforcement to acknowledge and reward positive behaviors can help build trust over time, especially for students who may have difficulty trusting authority figures.

Incorporating trauma-informed teaching practices, such as recognizing signs of distress and using calming techniques, can also benefit students who have experienced trauma. It's important to be flexible and open to adjusting your approach based on individual needs.

Providing emotional support is another crucial aspect of creating a trauma-informed classroom. This can involve fostering a supportive classroom culture where students feel comfortable expressing their emotions through activities like journaling or class discussions. It's important to recognize that some students may be hesitant to share their emotions openly, so providing alternative avenues for expression, such as anonymous suggestion boxes or one-on-one check-ins, can also be effective.

Collaborating with support services, such as school counselors, social workers, and other professionals, can enhance your ability to meet the unique needs of students who have experienced trauma. Recognizing that you may not have all the answers and seeking support from experts in trauma can benefit both individual students and the entire class.

By incorporating these teaching strategies and considerations, educators can create a trauma-informed classroom that promotes safety, trust, and support for all students. This approach contributes to a more inclusive and compassionate learning environment that benefits the entire school community.

Understanding a student's disabilities often allows individuals to view them with empathy, mirroring the way God might perceive them. This knowledge helps us recognize that the student may not always be in control of their behavior, fostering a sense of forgiveness and compassion. By embracing this understanding we become more empathetic and open to acknowledging the unique challenges these students face. Rather than seeing them solely through the lens of their disabilities, we are inclined to work collaboratively, offering guidance and support. It becomes apparent that, like everyone else, these students possess both strengths and weaknesses, but some of their challenges are beyond their control.

Approaching these students through the eyes of God involves seeing them not as broken or incomplete but as perfect creations with unique qualities and potential blessings. Recognizing the inherent value in each student contributes to a positive and inclusive learning environment.

Reflecting on personal experiences, learning about a student's disability has allowed me to practice greater empathy and forgiveness. For instance, gaining insight into the challenges a student faced due to their disability enabled me to appreciate their efforts and progress more deeply, fostering a more supportive and understanding relationship.

In terms of general strategies beneficial for all students, regardless of their disabilities, implementing consistent and predictable schedules is crucial. This provides a sense of routine and security. Offering both verbal and visual instructions caters to diverse learning styles, ensuring better comprehension. Employing multiple modes of instruction accommodates varied learning preferences, enhancing overall engagement. Establishing safe spaces within the classroom allows students to manage stress or sensory challenges effectively.

As educators, adopting these practices not only supports students with disabilities but also contributes to a more inclusive and effective learning environment for all. Seeing students through the lens of understanding and empathy, much like how God might view them, enriches the educational experience for everyone involved.

Reflective Questions

Reflect on the students who might challenge you the most. How can you be more intentional about showing them that you value their presence in the learning community?

_____

_____

In what ways can you incorporate the recommended teaching strategies and considerations into your interactions with students with disabilities?

_____

_____

How might you adjust your approach to better foster trust, especially with students who may have experienced trauma?

_____

_____

CHAPTER 5

COPING WITH CHALLENGES
AND CELEBRATING

It's essentially impossible to see the beauty in the ocean if you are drowning. Therefore, we need to make sure we are taking care of ourselves, our mental state, in order to love our students like God loves them.

Teaching is a profession that entails a range of complexities that require navigational skills to overcome. As educators, teachers face a multitude of challenges, such as managing challenging students, handling administrative tasks, and keeping up with the demands of the profession. Nonetheless, with the right mindset and approach, these difficulties can be addressed and resolved effectively. In this regard, this peace offers insights on how teachers can cope with challenges, celebrate victories, and build a community that supports their professional and personal growth.

It's essentially impossible to see the beauty in the ocean if you are drowning.

Coping with Challenges

> Consider it pure joy, my brothers and sisters, whenever you face trials of many kinds, because you know that the testing of your faith produces perseverance. Let perseverance finish its work so that you may be mature and complete, not lacking anything" (James 1:2–4)

Coping with challenges requires a combination of perseverance, mindfulness, and support from colleagues. Drawing inspiration from James 1:2–4, teachers can perceive challenges as opportunities for personal and professional growth. The testing of one's teaching methods or patience with difficult students can lead to perseverance and ultimately contribute to becoming a more effective educator. Additionally, practicing mindfulness can help teachers stay present in the classroom and manage stress. Prioritizing self-care is crucial for maintaining the energy and enthusiasm needed to address challenges effectively. Furthermore, building a supportive community among fellow teachers is vital. Sharing experiences and seeking advice from colleagues can provide valuable perspectives and coping strategies. Collaborative problem-solving fosters a sense of unity and shared responsibility. Open communication with school administrators is also key. When facing challenges with workload or administrative tasks, expressing concerns and working together to find solutions can help alleviate stress. Establishing a positive relationship with administrators contributes to a healthier work environment. It's not uncommon for us to disguise our complaints as requests for assistance, blurring the lines between seeking help and merely venting our frustrations. However, it's crucial for us to discern between the two: while griping and complaining may offer temporary relief, complaints seldom contribute to resolving the underlying issues. The act of expressing our concerns can be

53

cathartic, but true resolution comes from actively collaborating with those around us to find viable solutions. When we openly communicate our challenges and engage in a constructive dialogue, we create an environment that fosters problem-solving. Rather than dwelling on the negative aspects, we shift our focus toward understanding the root causes and working collaboratively to address them. In doing so, we not only find effective solutions but also alleviate the mounting stress that accompanies unresolved issues. The key lies in transforming complaints into opportunities for growth and improvement. By embracing a proactive approach and involving others in the process, we empower ourselves to navigate challenges successfully, fostering a culture of collaboration and resilience.

> But he said to me, "My grace is sufficient for you, for my power is made perfect in weakness." Therefore, I will boast all the more gladly about my weaknesses, so that Christ's power may rest on me. That is why, for Christ's sake, I delight in weaknesses, in insults, in hardships, in persecutions, in difficulties. For when I am weak, then I am strong. (2 Corinthians 12:9–10)

In order to successfully navigate the myriad of challenges faced by educators today, it is imperative to adopt a multifaceted approach that encompasses both practical strategies and a positive mindset. Fortunately, there are several effective techniques that educators can employ to not only overcome these challenges but to thrive in the education industry.

One of the most important factors for educators is effective time management. This includes prioritizing tasks, creating a schedule that incorporates specific time blocks for essential responsibilities, and setting achievable goals for both oneself and students. By breaking larger tasks into smaller, more manageable steps, educators can avoid feeling overwhelmed and maintain a sense of structure and control.

Another critical factor is building a strong support system through collaboration and networking. This involves cultivating positive relationships with colleagues, attending professional development workshops and conferences, and participating in mentorship programs to benefit from the guidance and experience of seasoned educators.

Flexible teaching strategies are also crucial to overcoming challenges in the education field. Educators must be adaptable and willing to adjust their approach based on the needs of their students and the dynamics of the classroom. This includes tailoring teaching methods to accommodate diverse learning styles and abilities, as well as exploring and integrating educational technology tools that can enhance teaching and streamline tasks.

Effective classroom management is also key, and includes establishing clear and consistent rules and expectations, using positive reinforcement to celebrate students' achievements, and developing conflict resolution strategies that encourage open communication to resolve issues and maintain a positive atmosphere.

Finally, self-care practices such as maintaining a healthy work–life balance, incorporating mindfulness and relaxation techniques into one's routine, and taking regular breaks throughout the day are essential to ensuring resilience and longevity in the education industry. Effective communication with parents and establishing a feedback loop with students can also aid in navigating challenges and fostering a supportive network.

Educators can enhance their resilience and effectiveness in addressing the diverse challenges that arise in the field of education by taking care of themselves and utilizing effective strategies. Regularly reflecting on teaching methods and classroom dynamics and developing a professional growth plan that includes specific goals for enhancing teaching skills can also positively impact educators' ability to navigate these challenges. With these strategies in place, educators can overcome obstacles with confidence and maintain a fulfilling and rewarding career in the education industry. When we feel fulfilled with our work, it is much easier to see the positive things around us. Therefore, we are more likely to see our students more like God sees them.

Celebrating Victories

Celebrating victories involves recognizing student achievements, setting and celebrating teaching milestones, team recognition, and showcasing positive classroom culture. Celebrating academic and personal achievements of students, no matter how small, is essential. Acknowledging their successes fosters a positive learning environment and motivates students to continue putting in effort. Teachers can also set personal and professional goals, breaking them down into achievable milestones. Celebrating these milestones, such as successful lesson plans or improved student engagement, helps maintain a sense of accomplishment and job satisfaction. Acknowledging and celebrating the achievements of colleagues fosters a sense of camaraderie. This could include recognizing innovative teaching methods, collaborative projects, or other contributions to the school community. Sharing positive aspects of the classroom environment with parents, administrators, and the broader community reinforces the importance of education. This can include highlighting successful student projects, engaging classroom activities, or testimonials from students and parents.

As an educator, one of the most powerful ways to create a positive and supportive learning environment is by celebrating the little things. Recognizing small achievements, efforts, and moments of growth can significantly boost morale, foster a sense of accomplishment, and contribute to a positive classroom culture. There are numerous creative and professional ways to celebrate these small victories, including:

1. **Verbal Acknowledgments**

    Providing individual praise that is specific and genuine for small achievements, improvements, or positive behaviors is an excellent way to acknowledge the effort and hard work students put into their tasks. Shout-outs to the entire class for positive group behavior, teamwork, or meeting a collective goal are also beneficial.

2. **Interactive Celebrations**

    Incorporating short, celebratory brain breaks into the lesson plan is an excellent way to celebrate small successes. These breaks could include a quick dance, a fun game, or a moment of shared laughter. Similarly, "theme days" that recognize and celebrate small moments of positivity and creativity, such as a "Positive Attitude Day" or a "Creative Thinking Day," can also be effective.

3. **Visual Displays**

Creating a bulletin board or wall space dedicated to showcasing small achievements is an excellent way to celebrate these moments. Displaying notes, drawings, or symbols representing each student's success, as well as using visual progress charts or graphs to track and celebrate incremental progress in individual or group goals, provides a tangible representation of small victories.

4. **Positive Notes and Certificates**

Personalized handwritten notes or digital messages to students recognizing their small accomplishments, highlighting specific details to make the acknowledgment personal, is an excellent way to provide positive reinforcement. Designing and distributing certificates for small achievements, such as mastering a new skill, completing a challenging assignment, or demonstrating positive character traits, is also effective.

5. **Class Celebrations**

Organizing short and fun minute-to-win-it games or challenges to celebrate small successes collectively can be a creative and engaging way to mark accomplishments. Similarly, forming a circle where students take turns sharing something positive or appreciative about a classmate fosters a sense of community and celebration.

6. Interactive Feedback

Incorporating regular reflection sessions where students share their small victories and personal growth through discussions, journals, or digital platforms is an excellent way to promote a culture of support and celebration. Encouraging students to provide positive feedback to their peers also reinforces the idea of continuous improvement.

7. Surprise Rewards

Implementing random acts of kindness as a way of celebrating the little things, such as surprise notes of encouragement, small treats, or other gestures of appreciation, can be an effective surprise reward. Introducing mystery rewards for individual students or the entire class when a collective goal is achieved can also add excitement to the celebration.

8. Inclusive Celebrations

Developing simple class cheers or chants that celebrate small victories is an excellent way to uplift the mood and create a sense of unity. Embracing and celebrating the cultural diversity within the classroom and recognizing and appreciating the little things that make each student unique is also beneficial.

9. Digital Celebrations

In virtual or blended learning environments, using digital tools to send virtual high fives, thumbs-ups, or other positive symbols to acknowledge small achievements is an excellent way to celebrate these moments. Creating digital showcases where students can share and celebrate their achievements through presentations, videos, or online platforms is also effective.

10. **Student-Created Celebrations**

Empowering students to take the lead in planning and executing celebrations, such as organizing a mini-talent show, a showcase of projects, or a themed celebration day, is an excellent way to promote student involvement and a sense of ownership. Involving students in creating collaborative displays that highlight their small victories, such as a class mural, a display board, or a digital portfolio, is also an effective way to celebrate these moments.

By celebrating the little things, educators can create a positive and inclusive learning atmosphere that fosters a mindset of continuous improvement and reinforces the idea that every effort and achievement, no matter how small, is valued and celebrated. This in turn helps the students themselves feel valued.

Building a Community

As educators who share the same Christian faith, finding and connecting with fellow believers is an important aspect of professional development. Collaborating with other Christian educators not only strengthens spiritual connections but also provides a support system that can help navigate the challenges of teaching in a complex and constantly evolving field.

> And let us consider how we may spur one
> another on toward love and good deeds,
> not giving up meeting together, as some are
> in the habit of doing, but encouraging one
> another—and all the more as you see the day
> approaching. (Hebrews 10:24–25)

One of the main benefits of connecting with fellow Christian educators is the shared faith that creates a bond and a mutual understanding. This spiritual support system is based on a shared foundation of beliefs that allows for mutual encouragement, prayer, and support during challenging times. As colleagues who share the same faith, we can offer each other spiritual guidance and wisdom rooted in Christian principles to navigate the obstacles we face in our profession.

The integration of faith and teaching is another reason why connecting with other Christian educators is important. By collaborating to integrate Christian values and principles into our teaching practices, we can provide our students with a unified approach to education that reflects our shared values and beliefs. We can also foster kindness, compassion, and respect within the school community and model Christ-like behavior for our students.

Furthermore, connecting with fellow Christian educators enables regular prayer support. This community of believers can come together to pray for each other, for students, and for the broader educational community. We can specifically pray for the well-being, spiritual growth, and academic success of our students. This shared commitment to prayer reinforces the sense of community and our reliance on God.

Accountability partnerships with other Christian educators can help maintain moral and ethical standards in the workplace. As colleagues, we can encourage each other to uphold Christian principles in our professional lives and lift each other up through words of encouragement, sharing testimonies, and affirming the impact of faith in our professional lives.

Overall, connecting with other Christian educators provides a unique opportunity for spiritual support, collaboration, and the integration of faith into the teaching profession. This shared foundation enhances the sense of community, contributes to a positive school culture, and allows colleagues to lean on each other for encouragement and guidance grounded in Christian principles. As Christian educators, it is important to remember that we are not alone and that together, we can create a powerful network of support and inspiration.

Implementing mentoring programs within the school provides support for newer teachers. Experienced educators can share insights, strategies, and coping mechanisms, fostering a sense of mentorship and community. Actively participating in school initiatives and committees allows teachers to contribute to the decision-making process. This involvement promotes a collaborative community where everyone's voice is heard and valued.

Navigating the complexities of being a teacher can be overwhelming. However, with perseverance, mindfulness, and a collaborative spirit, teachers can overcome challenges, celebrate victories, and build a resilient and supportive community within the educational environment. By implementing these approaches, teachers can foster an environment that encourages personal and professional growth, resulting in more effective educators who positively impact their students and the broader school community.

Teaching is an immensely rewarding profession, yet it also carries the burden of demanding responsibilities that often result in high levels of stress and burnout. As such, it is imperative that educators adopt effective stress management and self-care strategies to maintain a healthy work–life balance and a positive teaching environment.

One of the most critical steps to avoiding burnout is setting clear boundaries. By defining specific work hours and prioritizing moments of relaxation and personal activities, teachers can prevent burnout and maintain their physical and emotional health. Additionally, incorporating mindfulness and relaxation techniques such as deep breathing exercises into their daily routines can help them stay present in the moment and manage stress levels effectively.

Physical activity has proven to have many benefits for both physical and mental well-being, so it is essential that teachers integrate regular exercise into their routine. Whether it's a morning jog, yoga, or a workout session, physical activity can do wonders in alleviating stress and boosting energy levels. Furthermore, attending workshops or training sessions that focus on stress management and well-being can help teachers learn new strategies and techniques to cope with the challenges of the profession.

In order to cope with stress and burnout, teachers must also engage in self-reflection. By regularly reflecting on personal and professional goals, they can identify sources of stress and burnout, address them proactively, and make necessary adjustments. Establishing a support network among colleagues is also critical. Sharing experiences and challenges and seeking advice from others who may have faced similar situations, can provide much-needed support and perspective.

Additionally, many schools offer Employee Assistance Programs (EAPs) that provide confidential counseling services. Teachers can take advantage of these resources to discuss stressors and receive professional guidance. Ensuring that breaks and vacation time are taken regularly is crucial to preventing burnout as well. Taking short breaks during the school day and utilizing vacation periods for rest and rejuvenation can do wonders in recharging teachers' energy levels.

Recognizing small victories and moments of progress is also important. Encouraging teachers to reflect on their daily experiences and focus on positive moments and small victories can shift the focus from challenges to achievements. Acknowledging and celebrating small victories in student learning and behavior reinforces the impact of teaching and provides a sense of accomplishment. Additionally, establishing a culture of peer recognition within the school community fosters a supportive environment, and gratitude practices, such as keeping a gratitude journal, can promote a positive mindset and resilience in the face of challenges.

Taking action steps such as developing a personalized self-care plan, fostering a culture of open communication for collaborative problem-solving, advocating for resources and support, and promoting a positive school culture are all critical components of a holistic approach to stress management and self-care for teachers. By prioritizing well-being and recognizing both small victories and moments of progress, educators can build resilience and sustain a fulfilling career in teaching.

Within the field of education, educators are often faced with daunting responsibilities and challenges. However, the adoption of effective stress management and self-care strategies not only becomes a personal necessity but also a reflection of one's commitment to the well-being of students. By prioritizing these practices, educators enhance their own mental and emotional resilience while also gaining a unique perspective that allows them to view their students through the lens of compassion and understanding, much like how God might perceive His creations.

Intentionally taking steps toward maintaining a healthy work-life balance creates an environment where empathy and patience thrive. These virtues, rooted in self-care, allow educators to approach their students with renewed awareness and appreciation. Through the practice of mindfulness and relaxation techniques, teachers cultivate a space that encourages open communication, understanding, and a genuine connection with their students.

Clear boundaries are essential to creating a conducive learning environment. By setting these limits, educators safeguard their own mental and emotional well-being and demonstrate the importance of respecting personal boundaries to students. This modeling of healthy behavior becomes a powerful teaching tool, conveying the significance of self-respect and empathy in fostering positive relationships that extend beyond academic curriculum.

Regular physical activity and taking breaks are fundamental to maintaining physical health, and they also play a significant role in enhancing an educator's capacity for patience and empathy. These practices serve as tangible expressions of self-love and care, reinforcing the idea that teachers, too, are human beings with needs and limitations. In recognizing and addressing these needs, educators model understanding and acceptance, reflecting the way in which God looks upon His children with compassion and grace.

It is crucial to emphasize that these self-care practices not only benefit the individual educator but also have a profound ripple effect on the entire learning community. By embodying the principles of self-care, educators contribute to the creation of a nurturing and empathetic educational environment where students can thrive emotionally, socially, and academically.

The adoption and prioritization of effective stress management and self-care strategies in the realm of education is a transformative act that allows educators to view their students through the eyes of God—with love, understanding, and boundless compassion. In embracing these practices, educators become beacons of light, illuminating the path for their students to navigate life's challenges with resilience and grace. By recognizing small victories and moments of progress, establishing a support network, and taking action steps to prioritize well-being, teachers can build resilience and sustain a fulfilling career in teaching.

Reflective Questions

Consider your connection with fellow educators who share your same values. How do you currently find and connect with other Christian educators for mutual support and collaboration?

_____

_____

Reflect on your current stress management and self-care practices. Which strategies do you find most effective, and are there areas where you could make improvements?

_____

_____

Reflect on the action steps mentioned (i.e., developing a personalized self-care plan, fostering open communication, advocating for resources, and promoting a positive school culture). Which of these steps do you find most applicable to your current situation?

_____

_____

CONCLUDING PRAYER

Lord, I acknowledge that each student is uniquely created in Your image with distinct talents, challenges, and potential. In my quest to guide them, I pray for the insight to see them as You see them—with boundless love, infinite potential, and a purpose designed by Your divine plan. Help me to recognize and nurture the individual gifts they bring into the classroom, fostering an environment that celebrates diversity and encourages personal growth.

May Your love be a guiding force in my interactions with colleagues, fostering a sense of unity, collaboration, and shared purpose within the educational community. Let Your light shine through me, making me a beacon of encouragement and support.

Mold me into an instrument of Your peace, a conduit of Your wisdom, and a beacon of Your love within the realm of education.

I humbly present this prayer in Your sacred name, believing that through Your grace, I can fulfill the calling to be the educator You have created me to become.

Amen.

RESOURCES

*One learns from books and example, only
that certain things can be done. Actual
learning requires that you do those things.*

—Frank Herbert

Christian Educators
www.christianeducators.org

Christian Educators is a professional association dedicated to supporting, connecting, and protecting Christian educators working in schools. They aim to empower educators to serve as thriving ambassadors for Christ by providing support, connections, and relevant information. The company has launched "The Movement," a free community for educators to connect with peers, access daily devotionals and resources, stay informed about news and events, and receive a free legal freedoms overview.

Alliance Defending Freedom
www.adflegal.org

Alliance Defending Freedom (ADF) is an American conservative Christian legal advocacy group that champions the God-given right to live and speak the Truth. They engage in legal battles to protect religious liberty in schools. ADF receives numerous requests for legal aid annually. They work to uphold these freedoms through legal strategies, policy advocacy, and equipping their alliance with the tools to defend truth and religious freedom in law and public discourse.

_____'s Plan

Mindset into Actions

1. What is in my control?

_____

_____

_____

2. What do I need to do to see my students differently?

_____

_____

_____

3. How can I show love to the students who challenge me?

_____

_____

_____

4. How can I work to understand my students more?

_____

_____

_____

5. How can I celebrate strengths and victories?

_____

_____

_____

6. How can I take care of myself?

_____

_____

_____

7. Who can I connect with in my community and how?

_____

_____

_____

BIBLIOGRAPHY

Supply and Demand Report 2023 – Minnesota's State Portal. (n.d.). https://mn.gov/pelsb/assets/Supply%20and%20Demand%202023_tcm1113-562338.pdf

American Psychiatric Association. (2013). *Diagnostic and statistical manual of mental disorders* (5th ed.). https://doi.org/10.1176/appi.books.9780890425596

ABOUT THE AUTHOR

Alyssa Stickan is a passionate advocate for inclusive education and a dedicated professional with a rich background in special education. With a heart for embracing diversity, Stickan has brought her expertise to various settings, finding joy and inspiration in the unique challenges and differences within each one.

Having transitioned from the role of a special education teacher, Stickan now serves as an instructional coach, a pivotal role where she empowers and guides fellow special education teachers to reach their professional goals. Her journey from the classroom to the coaching sphere reflects a deep commitment to fostering an environment where every student, regardless of their abilities, can thrive.

Stickan's approach is characterized by a blend of empathy, creativity, and a relentless dedication to creating inclusive and effective learning environments. Her work extends beyond the classroom as she collaborates with educators to refine their teaching practices, overcome challenges, and champion the success of every student under their care.

In her pursuit of excellence in special education, Stickan continues to inspire and uplift her colleagues, shaping the future of inclusive education one classroom at a time.

Printed in the United States
by Baker & Taylor Publisher Services